MEGAHITS of 2012

13 Pop, Rock, Country, TV, and Movie Chartbusters

ARRANGED BY DAN COATES

Contents

Alfred

Produced by
Alfred Music Publishing Co., Inc.
P.O. Box 10003
Van Nuys, CA 91410-0003
alfred.com

Printed in USA.

ISBN-10: 0-7390-9356-8
ISBN-13: 978-0-7390-9356-6

 Alfred Cares. Contents printed on 100% recycled paper.

Boyfriend

Words and Music by
Mason Levy, Matthew Tyler Musto,
Mike Posner and Justin Bieber
Arranged by Dan Coates

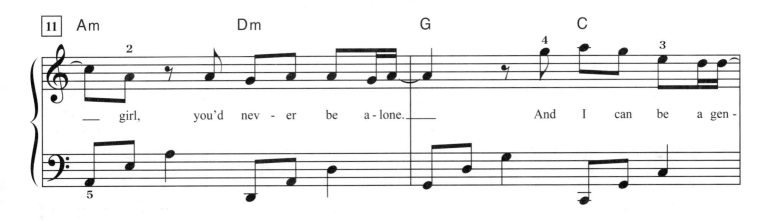

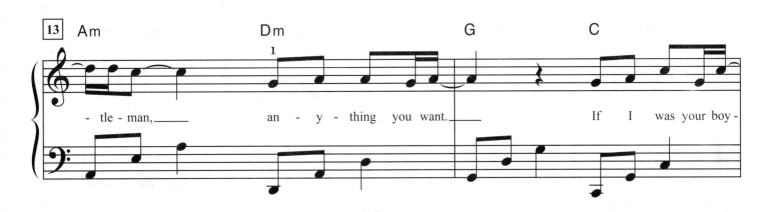

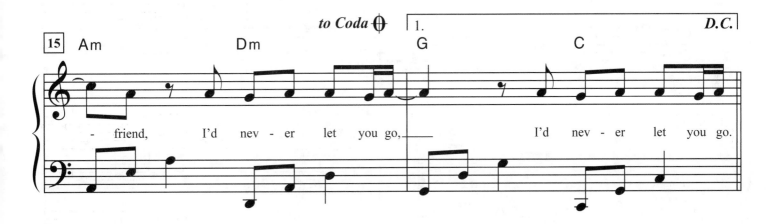

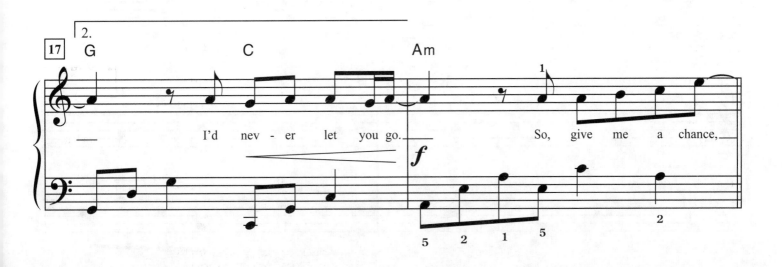

Verse 1 (rap):
If I was your boyfriend, I'd never let you go.
I can take you places you ain't never been before.
Baby, take a chance or you'll never ever know.
I got money in my hands that I'd really like to blow,
Swag, swag, swag, on you.
Chillin' by the fire while we eatin' fondue,
I don't know about me but I know about you.
So say hello to falsetto in three, two, swag.

Verse 2 (rap):
Tell me what you like, yeah, tell me what you don't.
I could be your Buzz Lightyear, fly across the globe.
I don't never wanna fight; yeah, you already know.
Imma make you shine bright like you're laying in the snow, brrr.
Girlfriend, girlfriend, you could be my girlfriend,
You could be my girlfriend until the world ends.
Make you dance, do a spin and a twirl, and
Voice goin' crazy on this hook like a whirlwind, swaggie.

The Big Bang Theory (Main Title)

Words and Music by Ed Robertson
Arranged by Dan Coates

Don't Stop Believin'

Words and Music by
Jonathan Cain, Neal Schon and Steve Perry
Arranged by Dan Coates

Verse 3:
A singer in a smoky room,
The smell of wine and cheap perfume.
For a smile they can share the night
It goes on and on and on and on.

Verse 4:
Working hard to get my fill.
Everybody wants a thrill,
Payin' anything to roll the dice
Just one more time.

Verse 5:
Some will win and some will lose,
Some were born to sing the blues.
Oh, the movie never ends,
It goes on and on and on and on.

Everybody Talks

Words and Music by
Tyler Glenn and Tim Pagnotta
Arranged by Dan Coates

Moderately fast

Verse:

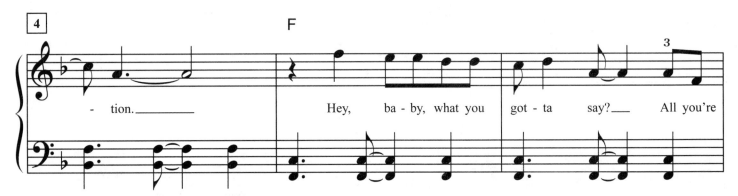

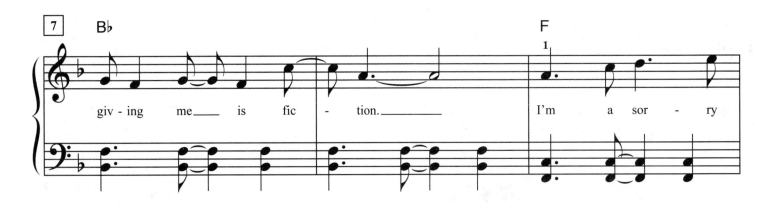

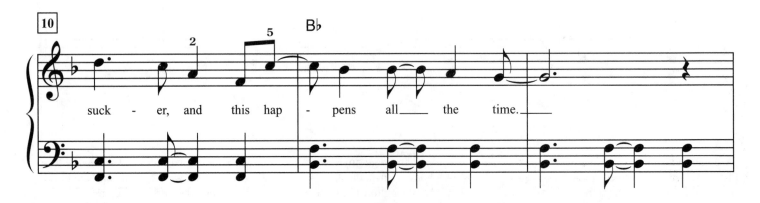

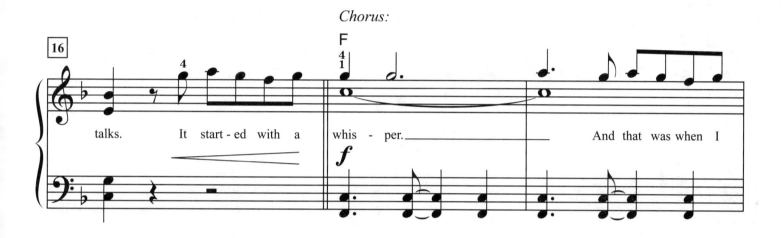

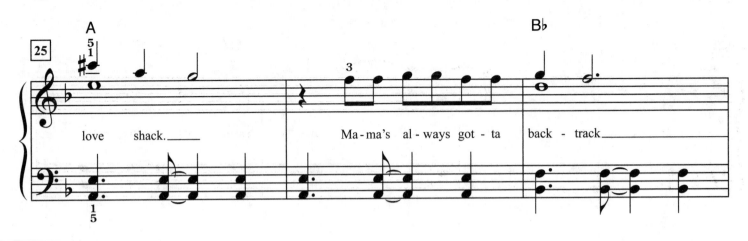

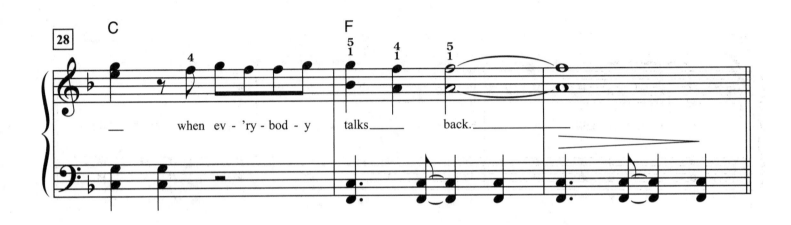

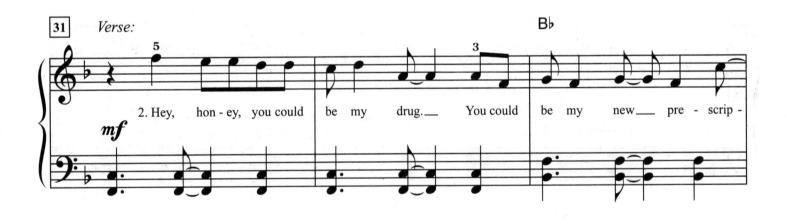

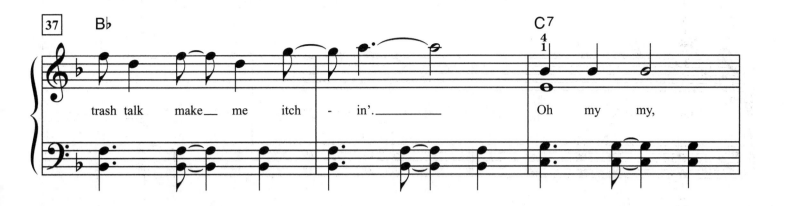

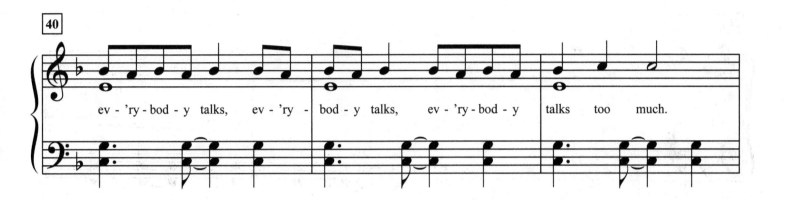

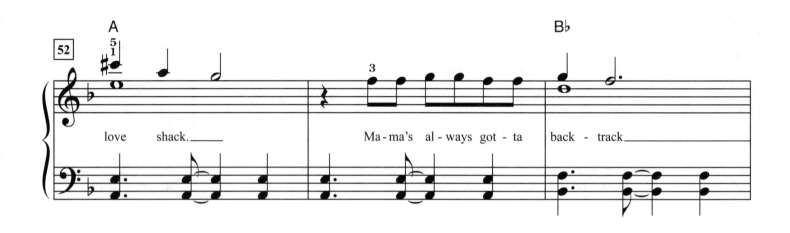

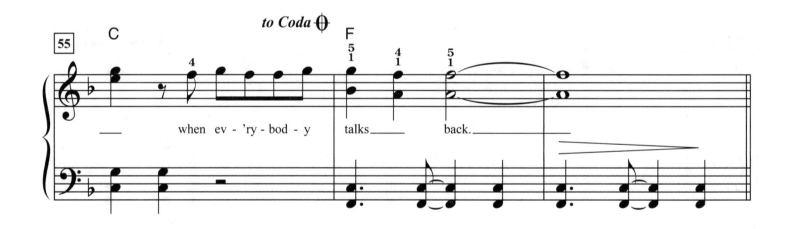

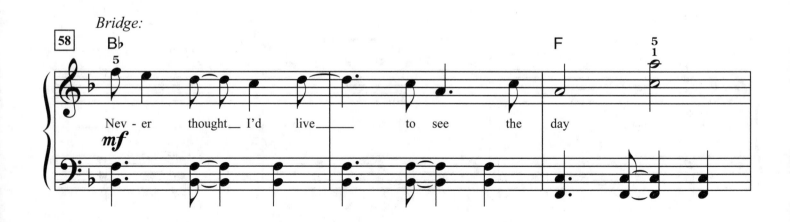

Falling Slowly
(from *Once: A New Musical*)

Words and Music by
Glen Hansard and Marketa Irglova
Arranged by Dan Coates

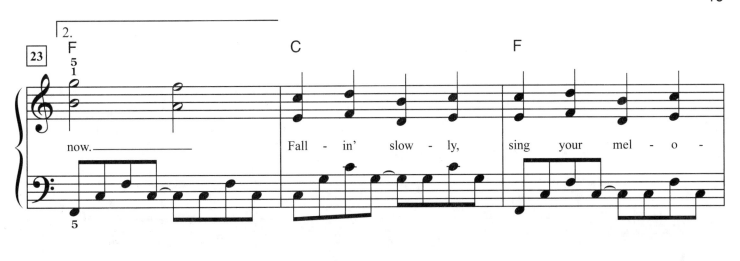

now. _____ Fall - in' slow - ly, sing your mel - o -

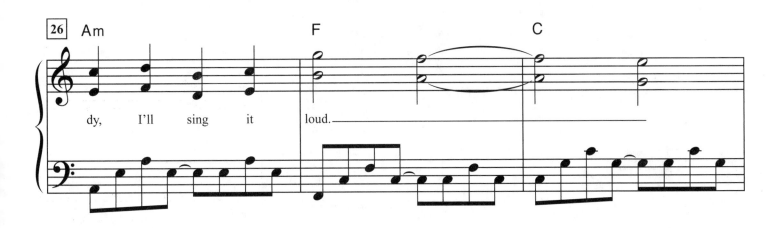

dy, I'll sing it loud. _____

Good Girl

Words and Music by
Carrie Underwood, Ashley Gorley and Chris DeStefano
Arranged by Dan Coates

Moderately, with a country rock beat

throw a - way the key.___ Hey,___ good girl, get out while you can.___ I

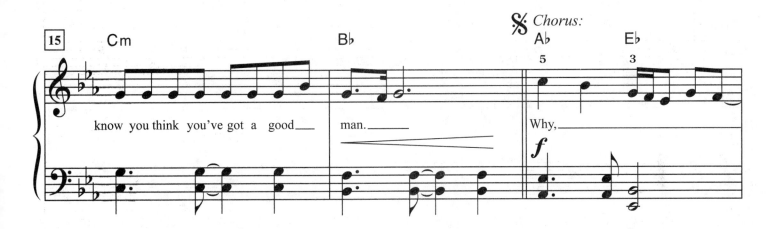

Chorus:

know you think you've got a good___ man.___ Why,___

___ why you got - ta be so blind?___ Won't you o - pen up your

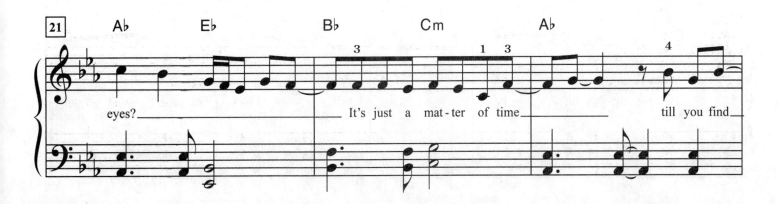

eyes?___ It's just a mat - ter of time___ till you find___

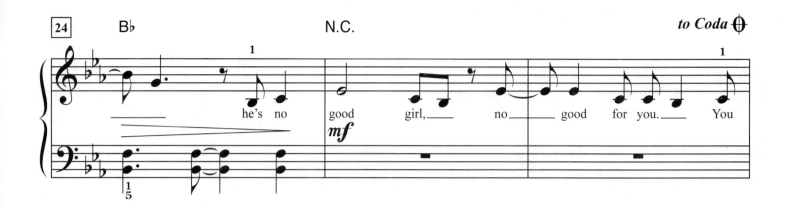

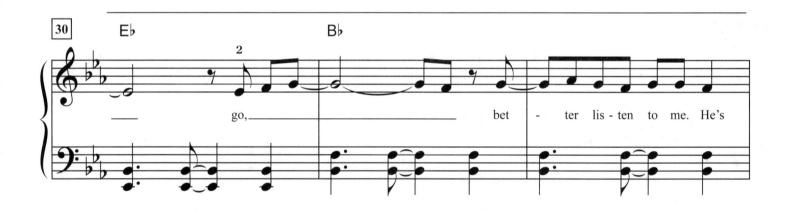

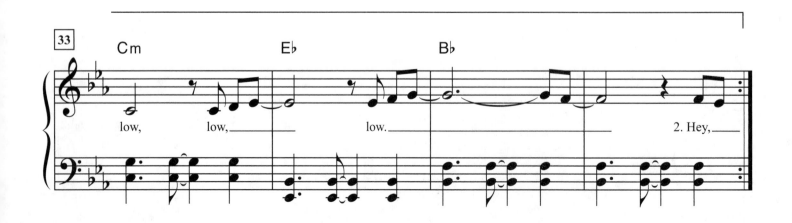

Verse 2:
Hey, good girl, you got a heart of gold,
You want a white wedding and a hand you can hold.
Just like you should, girl, like every good girl does,
Want a fairy tale ending, somebody to love.
But he's really good at lyin', yeah, he'll leave you in the dust,
Cuz' when he says forever, well it don't mean much.
Hey, good girl, so good for him.
Better back away honey, you don't know where he's been.
(To Chorus:)

Glad You Came

Words and Music by
Edward Drewett, Wayne Hector and Steve Mac
Arranged by Dan Coates

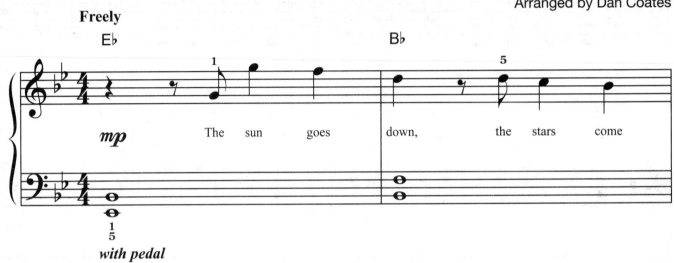

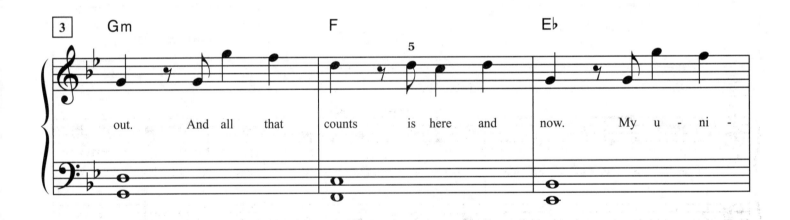

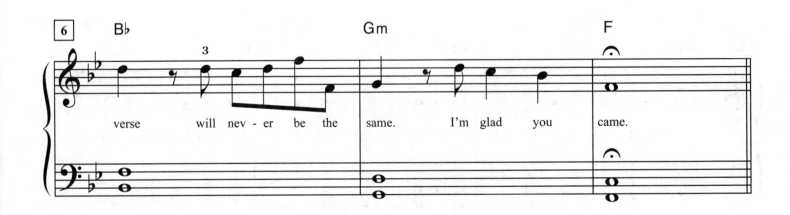

Brightly, with a steady beat

(2.) came.

mf

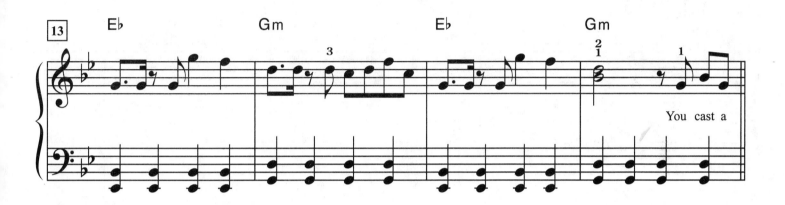

You cast a

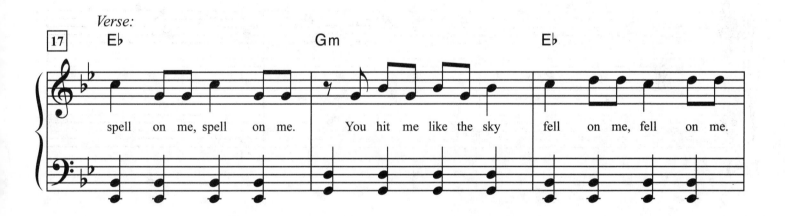

Verse:

spell on me, spell on me.   You hit me like the sky   fell on me, fell on me.

And I de-cid-ed you look   well on me, well on me.   So let's go some-where no one

else can see you and me. And turn the lights out now.__ Now I'll take you by the

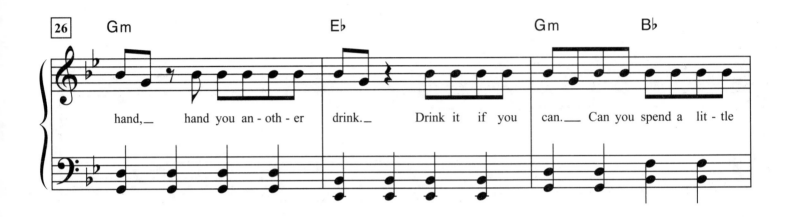

hand,__ hand you an-oth-er drink.__ Drink it if you can.__ Can you spend a lit-tle

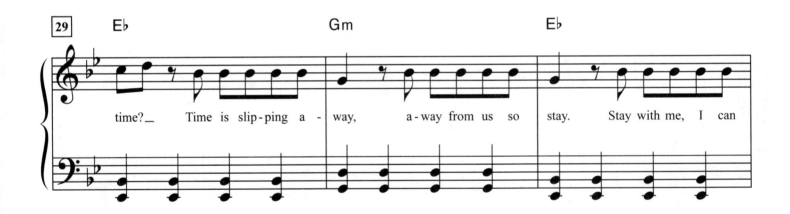

time?__ Time is slip-ping a-way, a-way from us so stay. Stay with me, I can

Chorus:

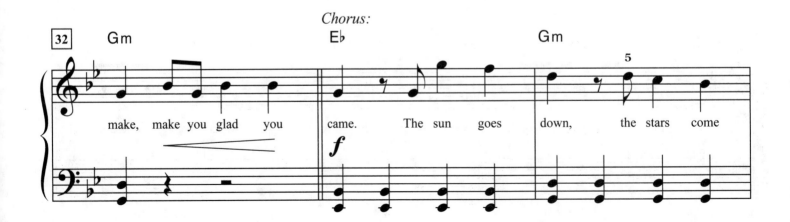

make, make you glad you came. The sun goes down, the stars come

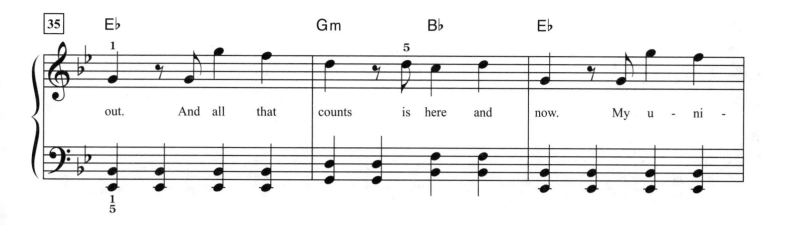

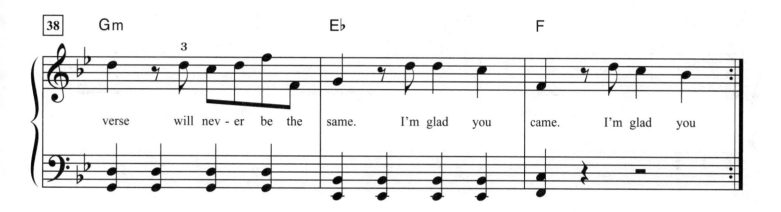

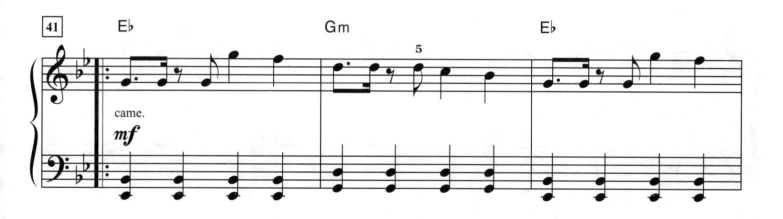

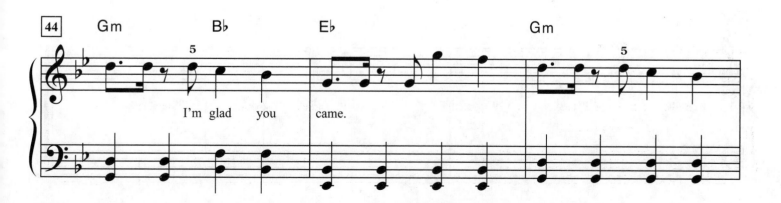

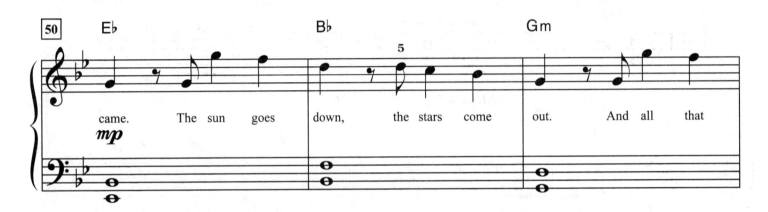

Payphone

Words and Music by
Wiz Khalifa, Adam Levine, Benjamin Levin,
Ammar Malik, Johan Schuster and Daniel Omelio
Arranged by Dan Coates

Moderately bright

I'm on a pay - phone try-in' to call home. All of my change I spent on you. Where have the times gone? Ba-by, it's all wrong. Where are the plans we made for two? Yeah, I,

Verse:

1. I know it's hard to re-mem-ber the peo-ple we used to be.
2. you turned your back on to-mor-row 'cause you for-got yes-ter-day.

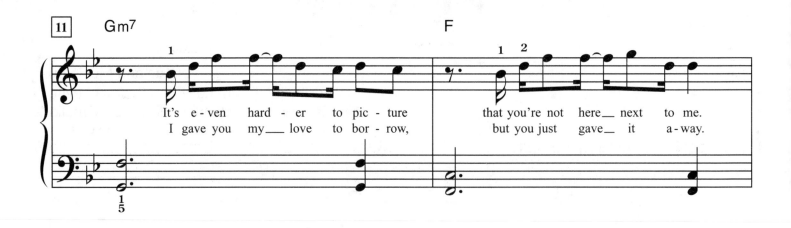

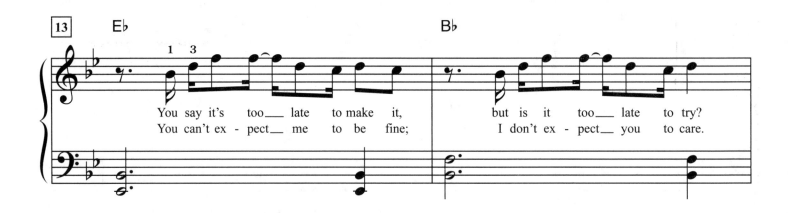

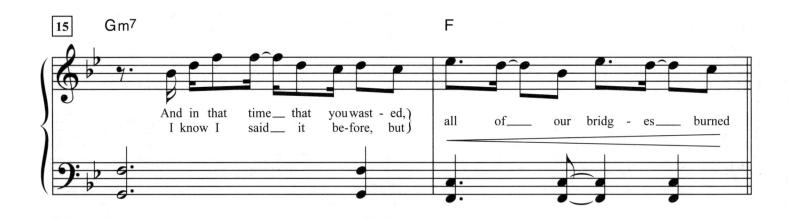

Pre-Chorus:

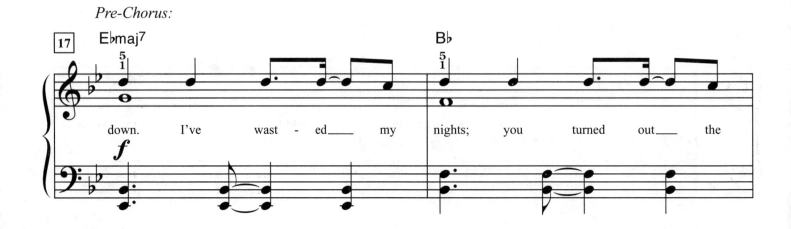

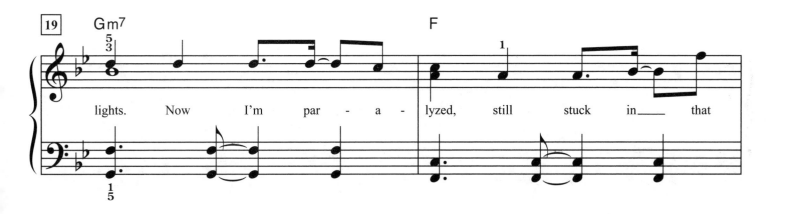

lights. Now I'm par - a - lyzed, still stuck in___ that

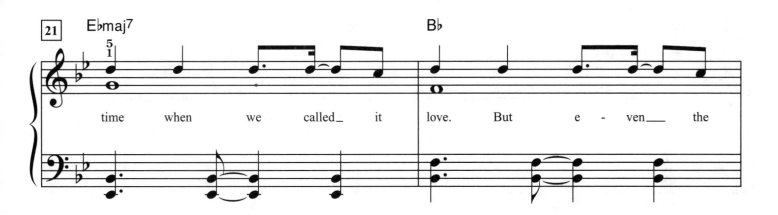

time when we called___ it love. But e - ven___ the

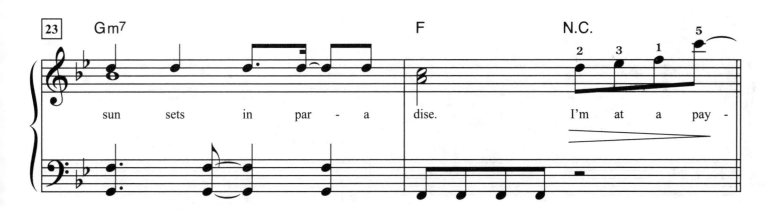

sun sets in par - a dise. I'm at a pay -

Chorus:

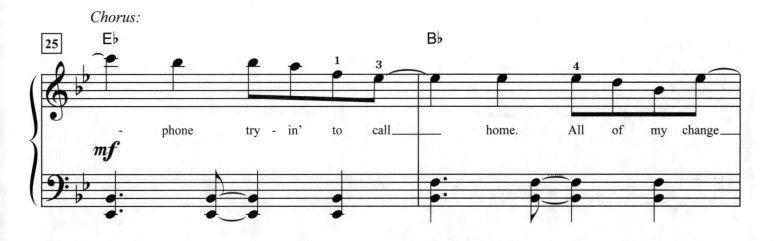

- phone try - in' to call___ home. All of my change___

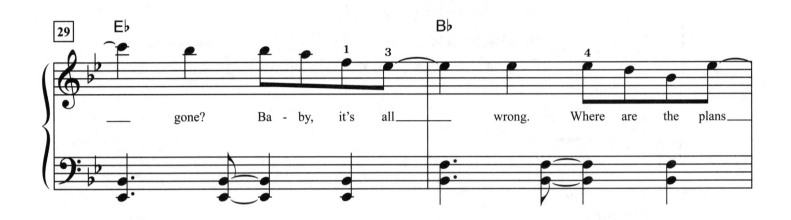

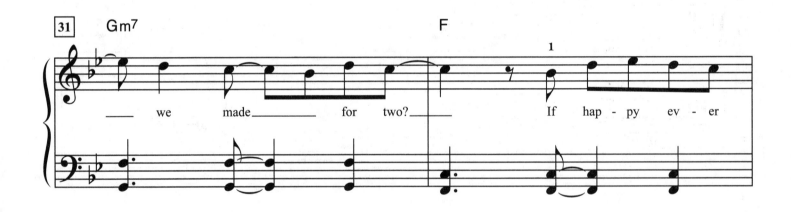

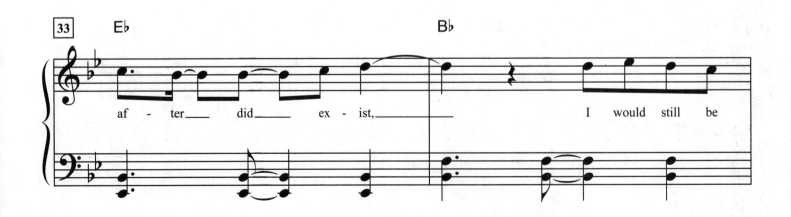

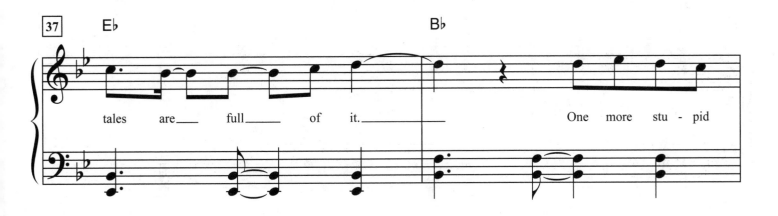

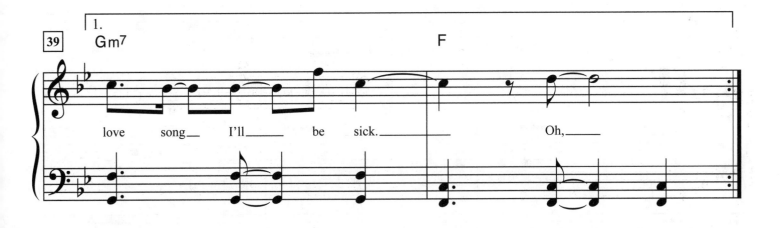

Some Nights

Words and Music by
Nate Ruess, Andrew Dost, Jack Antonoff and Jeffrey Bhasker
Arranged by Dan Coates

Moderately, with a steady beat

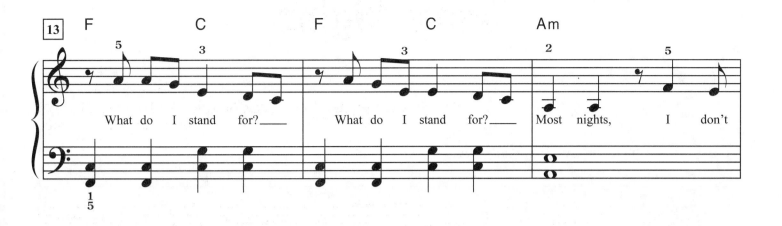

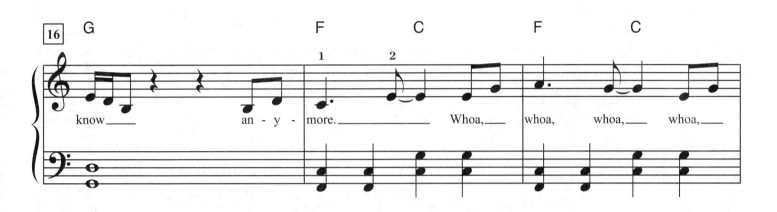

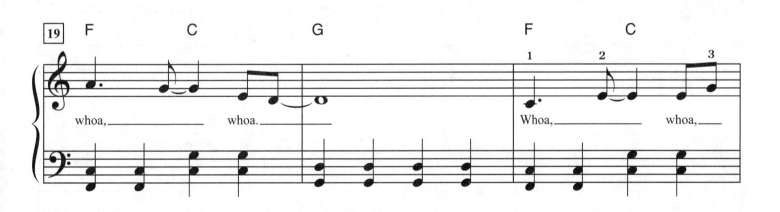

It's for the best we get__ our dis - tance, oh.__

__ It's for the best you did – n't lis - ten._____

It's for the best we get__ our dis - tance,__ oh.__

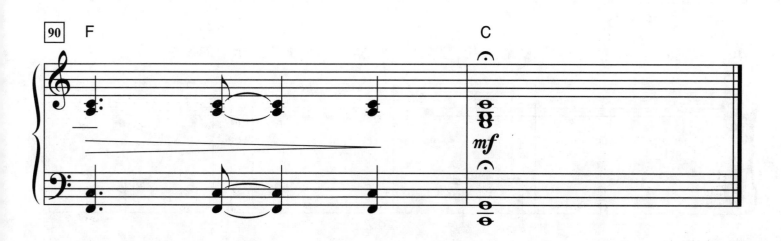

Secondhand White Baby Grand
(from *SMASH*)

Lyrics by Scott Wittman and Marc Shaiman
Music by Marc Shaiman
Arranged by Dan Coates

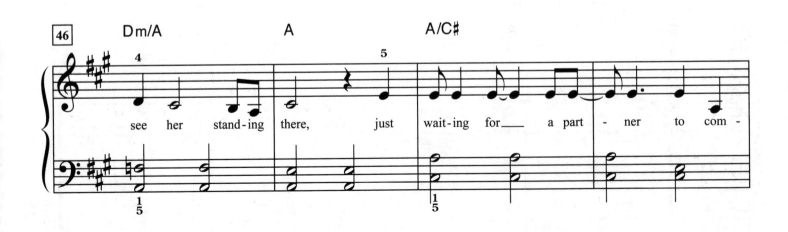

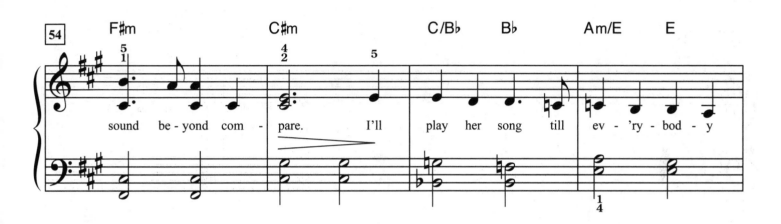

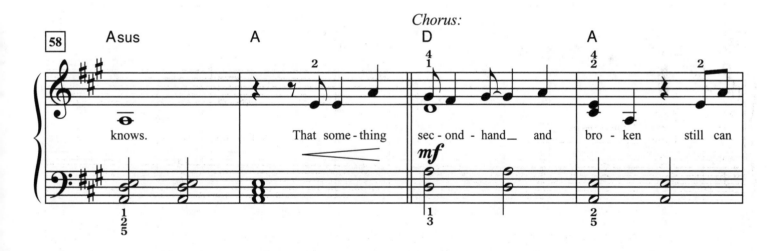

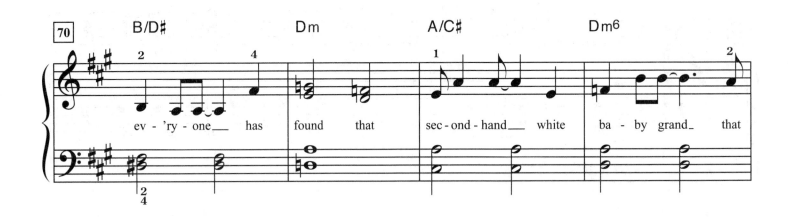

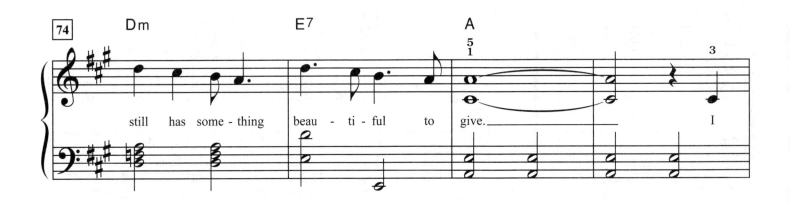

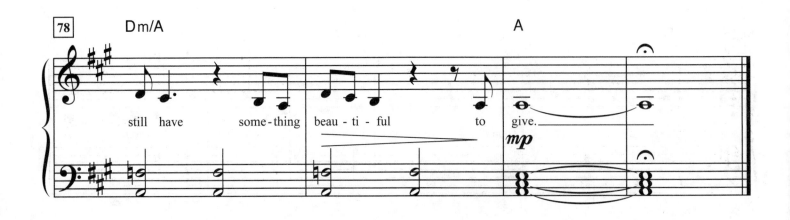

Tongue Tied

Words and Music by
Christian Zucconi, Hannah Hooper, Andrew Wessen,
Sean Gadd and Ryan Rabin
Arranged by Dan Coates

to Coda ⊕

loved you then, I love you now, oh, yeah.

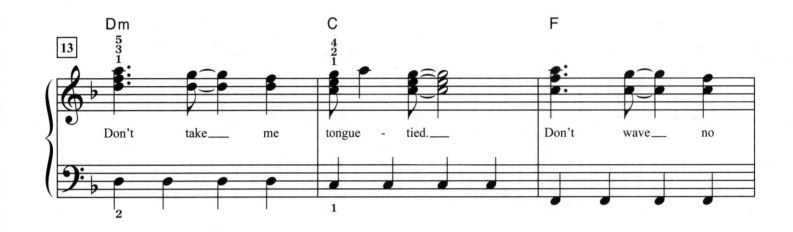

Dm   C   F

Don't take me tongue - tied. Don't wave no

Am7   Bb

good - bye.   Don't.

F

f

1.

2.

Don't leave me tongue - tied. Let's stay up all＿＿ night.

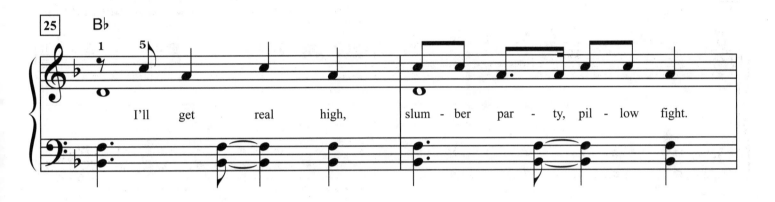

B♭

I'll get real high, slum - ber par - ty, pil - low fight.

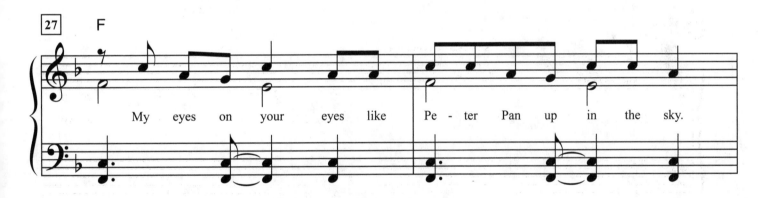

F

My eyes on your eyes like Pe - ter Pan up in the sky.

B♭

My best friend's house to - night, let's bump the beats till bed - dy - bye.

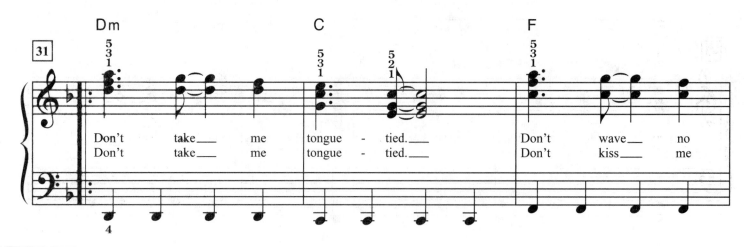

Don't take___ me tongue - tied.___ Don't wave___ no
Don't take___ me tongue - tied.___ Don't kiss___ me

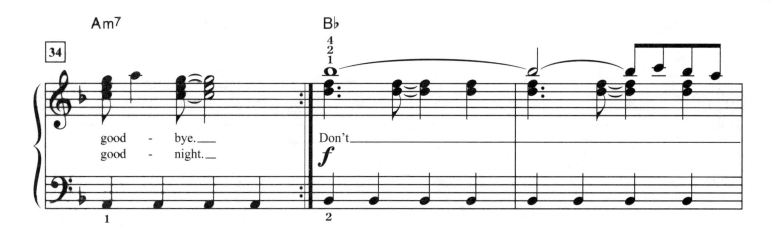

good - bye.___ Don't___
good - night.___

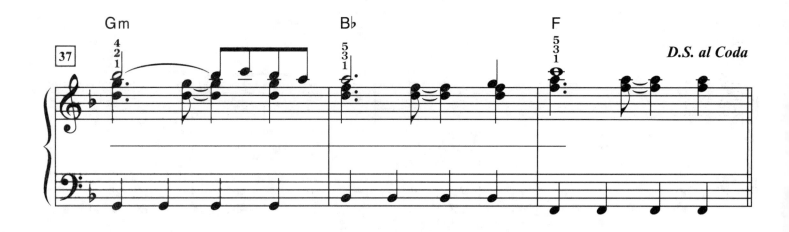

D.S. al Coda

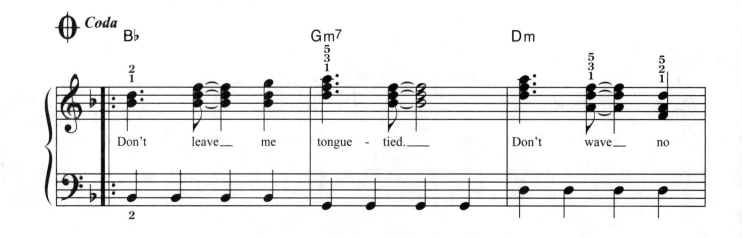

Coda

Don't leave___ me tongue - tied.___ Don't wave___ no

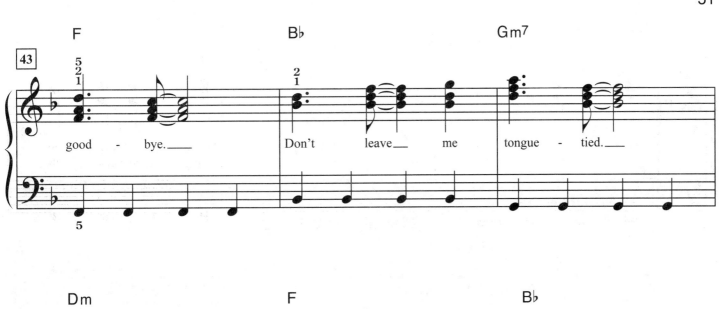

good - bye.____ Don't leave____ me tongue - tied.____

Don't.____

Yeah.____

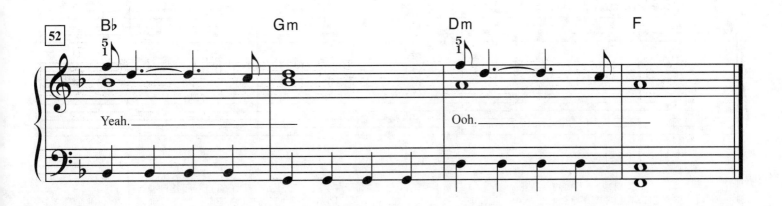

Yeah.____ Ooh.____

Wide Awake

Words and Music by
Katy Perry, Bonnie McKee, Lukasz Gottwald,
Max Martin and Henry Walter
Arranged by Dan Coates

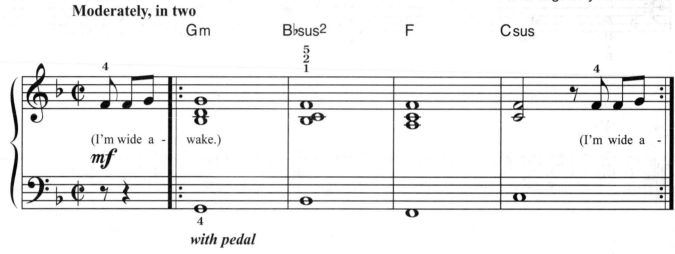

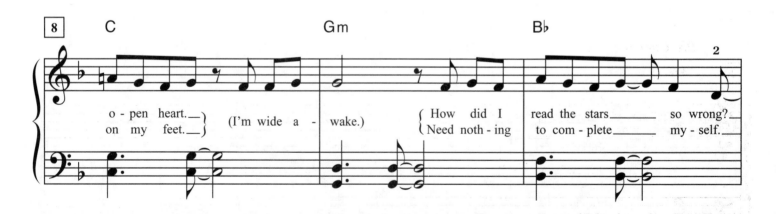

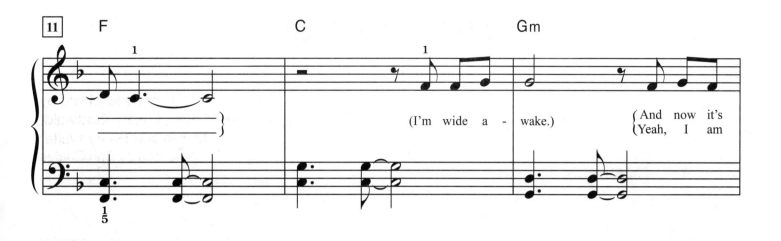

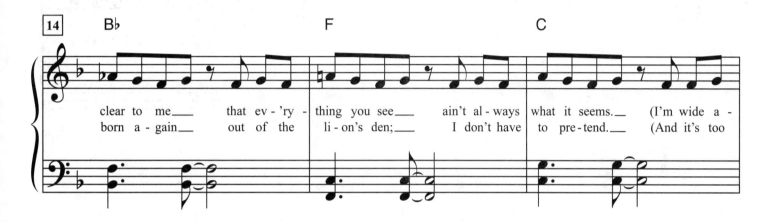

Pre-Chorus:

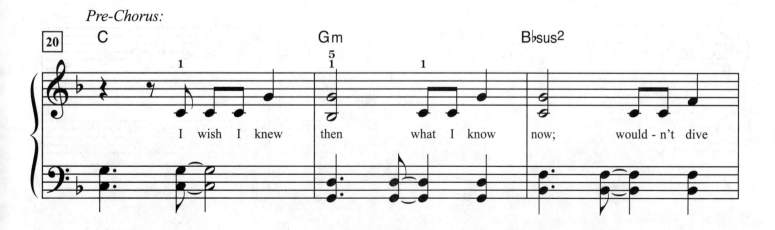

54

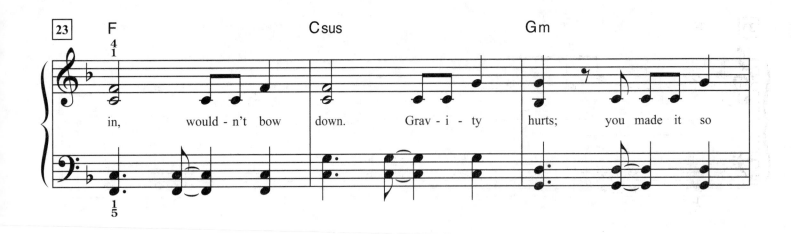

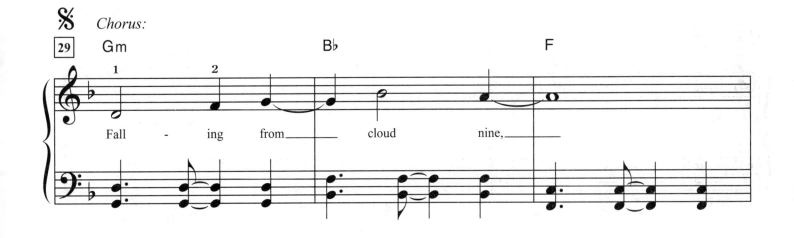

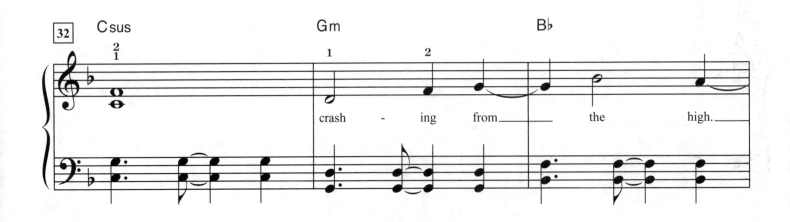

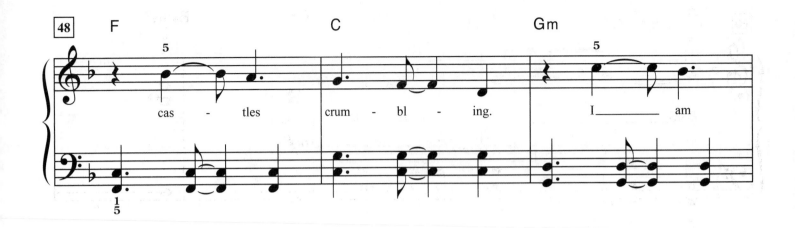

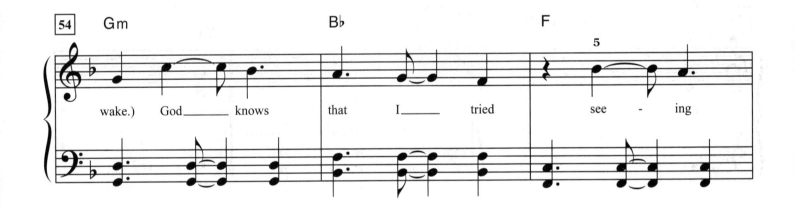

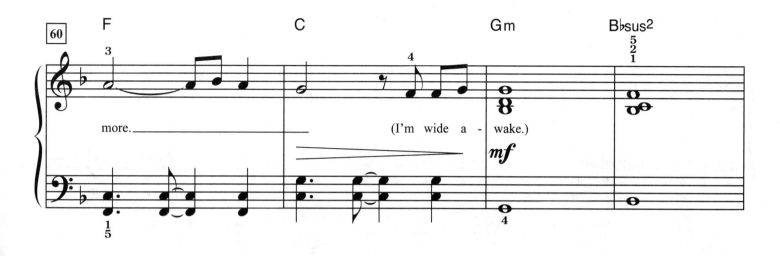

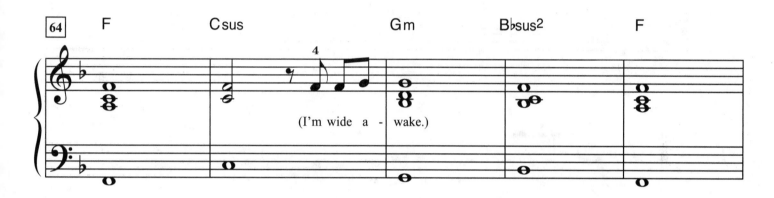

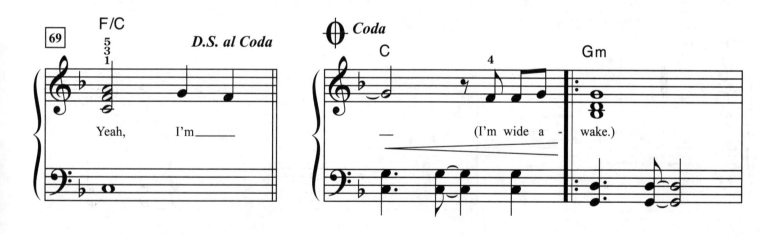

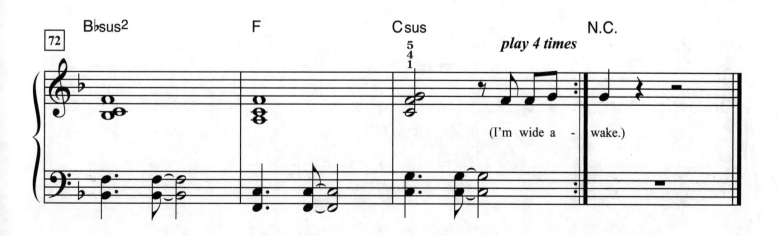

We Are Young

Words and Music by
Nate Ruess, Andrew Dost,
Jack Antonoff and Jeffrey Bhasker
Arranged by Dan Coates

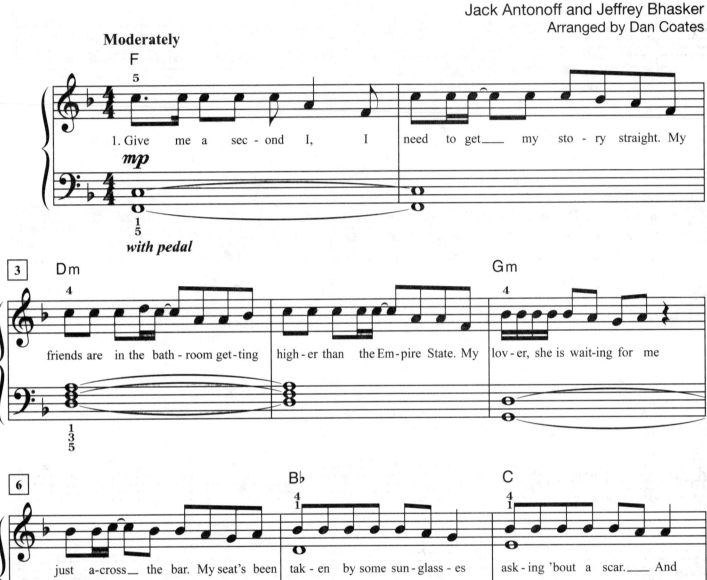

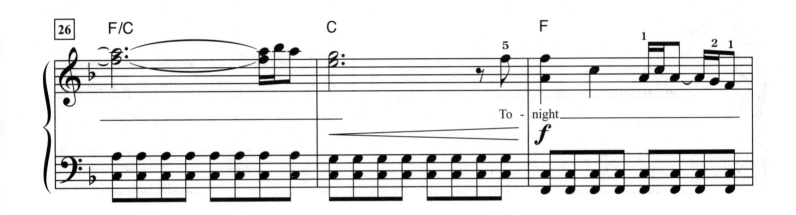

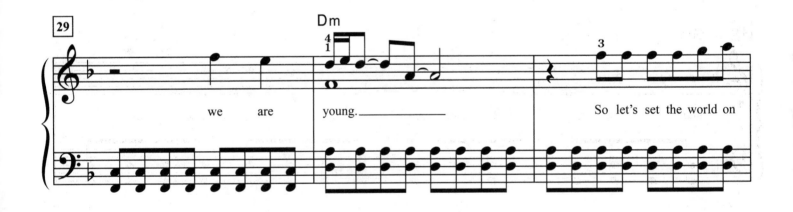

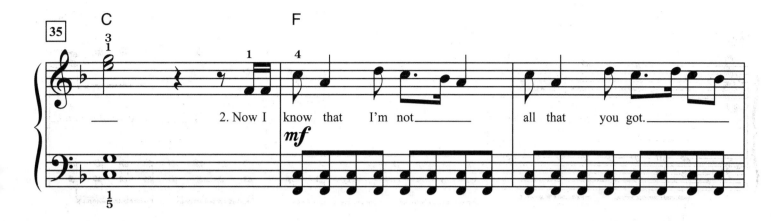

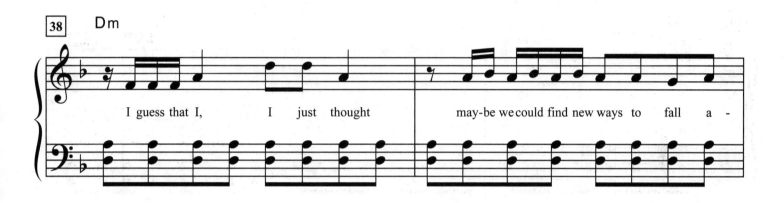

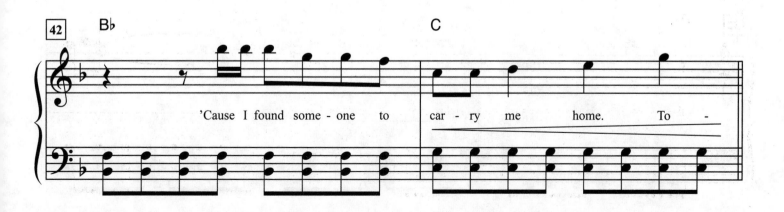

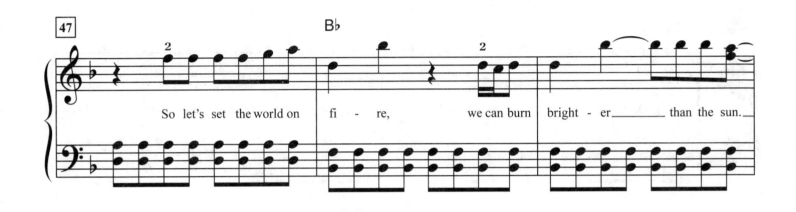

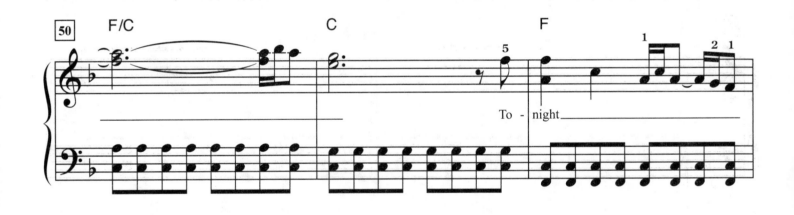

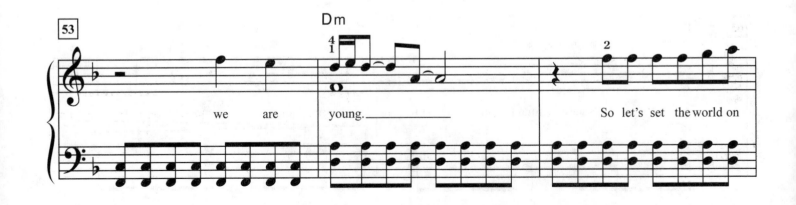

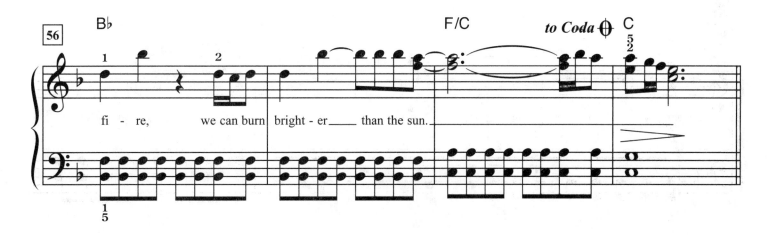

fi - re, we can burn bright - er____ than the sun.____

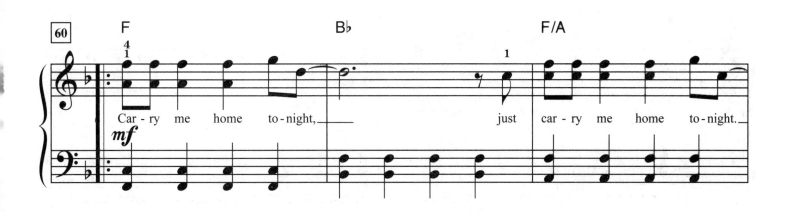

Car - ry me home to - night,____ just car - ry me home to - night.

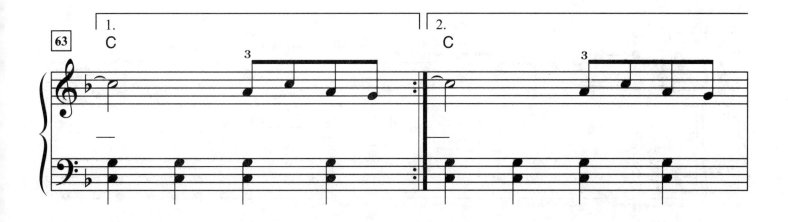

____ The world is on my side, I have no rea-son to run. So will some-one come and

carry me home tonight?___ The an-gels nev-er ar-rived,___ but I can hear the choir.

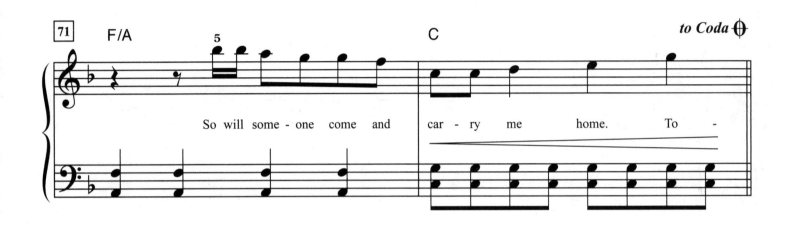

So will some-one come and car-ry me home. To -

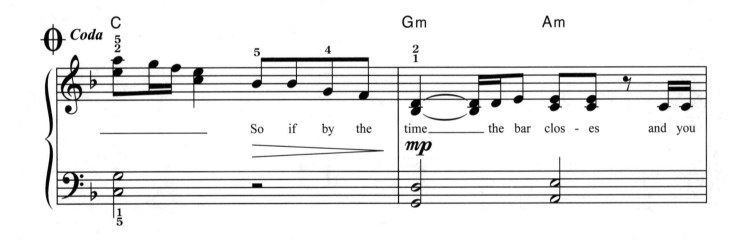

____ So if by the time___ the bar clos-es and you

feel like fall-ing down, I'll car-ry you home___ to - night.